THE KATHLEEN PARTRIDGE SERIES

Kathleen Partridge's Book of Flowers
Kathleen Partridge's Book of Friendship
Kathleen Partridge's Book of Golden Thoughts
Kathleen Partridge's Book of Tranquil Moments
Kathleen Partridge's Book of Faith
Kathleen Partridge's Book of Happiness
Kathleen Partridge's Book of Seasons
Kathleen Partridge's Book of Hope

First published in Great Britain in 1997 by
Jarrold Publishing Ltd
Whitefriars, Norwich NR3 1TR

Designed and produced by Visual Image, Craigend, Brimley Hill,
Churchstanton, Taunton, Somerset TA3 7QH

Illustrations by Jane Watkins

Edited by Donald Greig

ISBN 0-7117-0972-6

Printed by Proost, Belgium 1/97

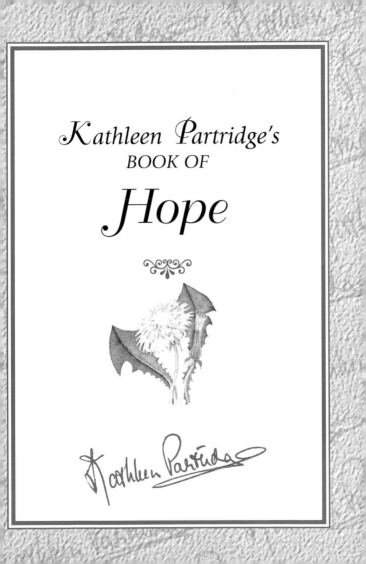

Kathleen Partridge's
BOOK OF
Hope

Tomorrow
Waits

We never can say at the end of the day:
'My work is accomplished, my duty is done.'
We never can say every hope has been realised,
Each plan is perfected, each aim has been won.

There is always a task or an incident pending,
A few threads of life that are lying untied,
An unfinished duty, some unwritten letters,
A muddle to clear, or a course to decide.

No matter how much has been done and forgotten,
How many decisions and plans have gone through,
There is just as much waiting for us on the morrow
Of problems unsolved and of tasks that are new.

For this is the way that life has to revolve,
There is never a full stop as long as we live,
There is the interest, this is the pleasure . . .
Something to take from life, something to give.

Daybreak

In the early hours of the morning
When the dawn is breaking through
There comes a lull in life
Before the day begins anew.

And then the birds start singing
Even louder with the light
As if their grateful voices
Plan to put the whole world right.

This is the hour to wake and wonder,
Fit your heart with wings that soar,
To buckle on your faith
And face whatever is in store.

Just for You

Make a brave new start today
As if the world were new
As if the dawn were breaking
Especially for you.

As if the singing rivers
Were rippling through your heart
Lift your spirits, lift your eyes
And make a brave new start.

Bluebell Time

Let me laze and let me linger
Though the world be in a hurry
Until I find the bluebells
In the sunny woods of Surrey.

They never fail or falter
Come what may in any year
I will waken one fine morning
And the bluebells will be here.

I scarce believe in Springtime
Till I gaze upon that view
Of so many little flowers
Massed to make the earth so blue.

Wooed by the Spring

Leaves that are bursting open
Daffodil buds uncurled
This is the giving of glory
The offer of gold to the world.

Wherever a garden is tended
Wherever a meadow is blessed
There will be daffodils dancing
By the kiss of the Spring caressed.

My Day

Say to yourself as you go on your way
I am going to be better and better today,
There's a purpose for living, a reason for fun
And I shall be friendly with everyone.

Say to yourself I refuse to frown
There is nothing so bad it can pull me down,
There are friendly faces and I shall see one
There are happy people and I shall be one.

Somebody Cares

There's never a singing river
Without solace in its song
And never a winding way
That travels uphill all along.

There's never a night so dreary
That dawn forgets to break
Nor time when someone does not smile
For someone else's sake.

Where God is

Upon the hill a Norman tower
Among the trees a spire
And cuddled down amid the town
A lych gate to admire.

A cathedral in the city
Or a meeting house of prayer
Each village street, or green retreat
Proclaims that God is there.

Why?

Why should we make the best of things
And look upon the bright side?
Why should we count our blessings
With a thought upon the light side?
Nobody can make us take
An optimistic view,
Nobody can make us,
But how pleasant if we do!

Why put ourselves to trouble
For friend or neighbour's sake?
Why seek for sympathetic words
When our heart doesn't ache?
We needn't show compassion
To another fellow man,
We are not bound to bother,
But how splendid if we can!

Flowers
of the
Future

These little brown husks in the palm of my hand
Are the flowers of the future that nature has planned;
I can blow them away and they'll fly far and wide,
But a few will take root in the fair countryside.

Here the secrets of life in these fragments remain
To be touched by the magic of sunshine and rain;
What colourful treasures are here in my keeping,
In the palm of my hand summer flowers are
sleeping.

For the Love of a Rose

Is it an angel's secret tears
In the heart of a rose when the dew appears,
Or the scroll that curls at the petal's edge
That talks of love and a lover's pledge?

Or is it the perfume, deep and sweet,
Where the loveliest hours of the summer meet
To lighten the heart and to ease the woes
And make us live for the love of a rose?

Bank Holiday

Blue water for serenity
White sails when hope runs high,
No finer sight to lift the heart
Than sails against the sky.

So make this day a holiday
From all the usual things.
Listen to the carefree songs
A bird in Summer sings.

Let no troubles cloud your view
No wilful words annoy,
Just sing a song for happiness
And say a prayer for joy.

Shadows

We are never surprised when the sun casts a
shadow,
In fact we can sit and admire light and shade;
We know that each street has a bright and a dull
side,
For that is the way that the world has been made.

Then why be astonished when life casts a shadow,
Obscuring the sun for a moment or two;
This is the way in the course of a lifetime
Of proving the joy and enhancing the view.

A walk in the shade never harms anybody,
It softens hard outlines and brings the heart grace;
Look for the beauty that rests in the shadows
Until the scene shifts and the sun takes its place.

Havest Festival

Although some seeds are wasted and some
work destroyed by gale,
Some crops yield unexpectedly, while others
seem to fail,
Yet there must be a harvest, the fulfilment of
our toil,
The goodness will be gathered after
patience from the soil.

*And life, too, has a harvest for the aims
that we pursue,
Although some good deeds planted do not
flourish it is true,
Some plans are disappointing, sown too
early or too late,
While impulses of kindness might grow
friendships that are great.*

*In nature and in life we plan our way and
sow our seeds,
But in God's time and season reap the
harvest of our deeds.*

The Garden at Dusk

In the cool of a garden when evening draws in
Serenity waits where the shadows begin,
In the fragrance of dusk and the murmur of clover
The cares that we carry pass peacefully over.

Flowers in the fullness shed blessings about
And the turmoil of living fades quietly out,
Hope glimmers through with the evening star
And anxieties shrink to the size that they are.

Evergreen

The yew is for sorrow, but green is the leaf
Keeping its foliage even in grief;
That is the reason why yews go not bare
But point to new hope in the midst of old care.

And evergreen colours are not born to die
But decorate earth when the summer goes by,
They cover the landscape while earth takes a rest
Immortal, heartlifting, and by our Lord blessed.

House Warming

Cold are the mornings and dark the night
But the glowing fires are a welcome sight,
Though branches sigh when the east wind blows
A Christmas tree in the window glows.

And Winter must change one day to Spring
Trees must blossom and birds must sing,
And clouds turn silver that looked so black
And all life's sunbeams be welcomed back.

The New Year

With time there is no turning back – roll
round another year,
The old one with its pangs and pains will
find no comrade here.

On towards adventure, facing all the
tracks we tread,
To shake hands with the future – proud
to meet what lies ahead.

With time, no turning back; with life, no
old regret nor fear,
Start fresh with zest and joy to meet the
new unsullied year.